DODD, MEAD WONDERS BOOKS

Non coelo tantum, sed et mari suae stellae sunt.
(Not only in heaven, but also in the seas are there stars.)

J. H. Linck, *De stellis marinis*, 1733

Wonders of STARFISH

Morris K. Jacobson and William K. Emerson

Illustrated with photographs and line drawings

DODD, MEAD & COMPANY · NEW YORK

To Kenneth and Elana

Acknowledgments

Illustrations on pages 24, 37, 40, 44, and 57 (right) are from *Echinoderms of Connecticut* by Wesley R. Coe, State Geological and Natural History Survey of Connecticut, Bulletin No. 19, Hartford, 1912.

Illustration on page 69 is from *Grzimek's Tierleben*, vol. 3, Bernhard Grzimek, ed., Kindler Verlag AG, Zürich, 1970. Reprinted by permission of the publisher.

Illustrations on pages 15, 27, 39, 42, 43, 48, and 71 are from *Kurs Zoologii*, G. G. Abrikosova and L. B. Levinsona, eds., Moscow, 1955.

We gratefully acknowledge the assistance of various kinds given us by Dr. David Pawson and Ms. Maureen E. Downey of the Smithsonian Institution, Drs. Arthur S. Merrill and Warren S. Landers of the U.S. Department of Commerce, National Marine Fisheries Service, and Dr. Alan J. Kohn of the University of Washington.

Picture Credits: American Museum of Natural History, pages 6, 9, 10, 13, 16, 18, 22, 29, 31, 34, 35, 46, 64, 66, 67; James D. Dunn, 26; Edward Forbes, 2 (frontis), 19, 57 (left); Ernst Kirsteuer, 49, 51; Arnold Ross, 28; Gunnar Thorson, courtesy of Ellen Thorson, 32; U.S. Department of Commerce, National Marine Fisheries Service, Milford, Conn., 23, 60, 61, 62; Westinghouse Electric Corporation, Ocean Research Laboratory, 17, 54; Poul H. Winther, courtesy of Ellen Thorson, 33.

1   2   3   4   5   6   7   8   9   10

Library of Congress Cataloging in Publication Data

Jacobson, Morris K
    Wonders of starfish.

    Bibliography: p.
    Includes index.
    SUMMARY: Describes the physical characteristics and habits of different species of starfish and discusses their relationship to other sea creatures and human beings.
    1. Starfishes—Juvenile literature. [1. Starfishes. 2. Marine animals] I. Emerson, William K., joint author. II. Title.
QL384.A8J3   593'.93   76–53584
ISBN 0–396–07416–2

CONTENTS

Starfish stranded at Orchard Beach, New York. Notice their trails in the sand and the specimen on the lower left trying to right itself.

1

Introduction to Starfish

Starfish are perhaps the most familiar of all the animals that dwell in the sea. Yet they are one of the strangest-looking of all living creatures. Their body plan and many of their anatomical features are utterly different from those of most other animals.

Their almost perfect, starlike shape immediately attracts the attention of anyone who is lucky enough to find one thrown up onto the beach by waves or stranded on the shore by retreating tides. Their attractive shape together with the ease with which specimens can be collected, dried, and preserved make them one of the most popular souvenirs of a visit to the seashore.

Mankind has long associated starfish with the sea. The Greek scholar Aristotle in the 4th century B.C. wrote interesting accounts of the ones living in the Mediterranean Sea. Starfish have been often pictured in drawings and wall decorations dating from ancient times, and today artists commonly feature them in beach or seashore scenes. They are even pictured on postage stamps and also serve as emblems on coins.

But what are starfish? The answer to this seemingly simple question requires a somewhat detailed explanation, and it is given in the following chapter. For the moment it is enough to say, that strange as they look, starfish are not the only animals of their kind. They are related to sea urchins and to several other similar kinds of creatures, all of which belong to a large group or phylum of animals called the echinoderms.

To us the common name, starfish, seems to be well chosen since many kinds have a starlike shape. But some zoologists prefer to use the name "sea star" because starfish are not true fish at all. Moreover, they point out that the French, Russians, Germans, and many other people use words which translate into "sea star." Perhaps this is a better name, but the use of "starfish" is so firmly fixed in our language that it would be difficult, if not impossible, to displace it. Actually there is no need to change the name as long as it is understood that starfish are not vertebrates, or animals with backbones, and they are not confused with the true fishes.

Starfish are found almost everywhere in the sea, from the intertidal zone and shallow coastal waters to oceanic depths of almost 6 1/2 kilometers (4 miles) beneath the surface. They live on rocky, sandy, or muddy bottoms, in icy polar waters, as well as in warm tropical seas. But they can live only in the oceans. In this respect they differ from many other kinds of invertebrates like the crustaceans (crabs, crayfish, sowbugs, and their kin) and the mollusks (clams, oysters, snails, and their relatives), some of which have become adapted to life in fresh water or even on dry land. Despite the fact that the starfish and the other echinoderms are limited to life in salt water, they are one of the oldest and most successful groups of all the invertebrates. The echinoderms as a group first appeared in the seas about 600 million years ago, and starfish made their appearance some 100 million years later. Thus starfish were here on earth more than a half billion years before human beings.

The most characteristic feature of starfish anatomy is the presence of starlike rays, also called arms. Typically there are five rays or arms, but many species have arms in multiples of five—15, 25, 45, and up to 50. Others have 6, 7, or 14, but there are few

The fragile pencil starfish (Thrissacanthias penicillatus) *lives in deep water off the west coast of the United States.*

normal four-rayed forms; one such lives in European waters, but none in North America. Thus any starfish with four arms found on North American shores is either a cripple or a freak of nature. The arms are mostly tapering and straight, some being quite short and others long and narrow. One group of starfish seem to have no arms at all and look like five-cornered cookies or peculiar little pincushions.

Starfish range in size from tiny creatures no more than 2 centimeters (4/5 inch) from arm tip to arm tip, to one giant in the north Pacific which can reach a width of 1.3 meters (more

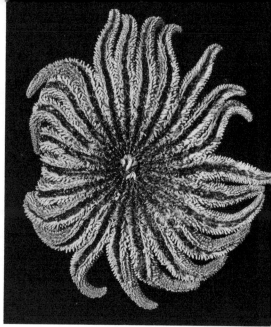

Top and bottom views of the sunflower starfish (Pycnopodia helian-
thoides), *the largest known starfish. It lives offshore and intertidally,
where it frequents oyster and clam beds, from Alaska to California.*

than 4 feet). Most species, however, are moderate in size, varying from about ten to 30 centimeters (4 to 12 inches) across. The
upper surface is hard and usually ornamented with hooks, warts,
granules, and spines. Other species have long, sharp, poisonous
spines.

Starfish are commonly colored in tones of red, orange, or
brown, but these colors are generally subdued. However, in
others the color is quite brilliant. In these we find vivid shades of
green, violet, purple, blue, and gray. Some have more than one
color and are mottled or speckled in different shades—red or
purple, with white or yellow specks often arranged in uneven
but attractive designs. Often a single species will have individuals of different colors. The blood starfish (*Henricia sanguin-
olenta*) of northern seas, for example, is usually bright red or
orange, but cream-colored, yellow, pink, and purple specimens
are also found. One writer declared that a glass dish filled with an

10

assortment of these starfish alive would be as beautiful as a bed of tulips because of the brightness and variety of their colors. One species called *Crossaster papposus* (meaning "downy fringed star") belongs to a group known as sun stars because they all have many conspicuous arms. The entire upper surface of these starfish is so colorful that it looks like a sunburst. They are thought to be the most beautiful of all echinoderms.

Starfish may have a surprising appearance, but many of their ways of living are even more so. We shall describe the unique water vascular system that enables them to walk and climb, the fantastic way they capture and eat their food, and the peculiar methods some use to care for their young. We shall also explain why they flourish, their unusual internal skeleton, and the external organs that serve to protect them—organs which are found only in the starfish and their closest relatives. And finally we shall show that in spite of seeming to be harmless and inoffensive creatures, many are actually voracious carnivores. They kill and eat vast numbers of clams, oysters, and scallops—food which we humans would prefer to keep for ourselves. They also can attack and devour snails, crabs, other starfish, and fish. Some even destroy coral reefs. In short, they can consume almost any living thing in the sea, dead or alive, which they can find and swallow. Their presence causes many creatures to use all sorts of ways to avoid them. We will describe some of these escape responses later in this book, and we will also say something about the huge losses starfish can cause oyster farmers and the more or less successful, but always expensive, means oystermen must use to control them.

After learning about starfish, and how to collect, preserve, and identify them, perhaps you will want to keep one at home in a saltwater aquarium. With patience, you should be able to observe your pet feeding when it extends the stomach out of its mouth and into the open valves of a living clam.

2

Characteristics and Classification of Starfish

One of the most noticeable things about starfish is that they do not have a front or a back; for that matter, neither do they have a left side or a right side. Any one of the five or more arms or rays can be front, left side, right side, or back in turn, for starfish are built on what is called a round or *radial* plan. In the center, they possess a flat, round, platelike disk called the *central disk*. The central disk is divided usually into five sections, from each of which generally one or more raylike arms extend out like the spokes of a wheel. Since these more or less equal arms radiate at almost regular intervals, the starfish body is said to be symmetrical, that is, even and regular, and the body is described as being *radially symmetrical*. On the other hand, most animals exhibiting true front and back ends have the body divided into similar-looking right and left sides. In these, the body is alike on both sides of an imaginary dividing line running down the center, and the animals are said to be *bilaterally* (two sidedly) *symmetrical*. Several other invertebrates like sponges, coral polyps, sea anemones, and jellyfish also have radial symmetry, but most larger animals, with or without a backbone, are bilaterally symmetrical. (We humans, of course, are bilaterally

Top and bottom views of the eleven-rayed sun star (Solaster endeca), *which usually has nine to eleven rays and occurs in the northern Pacific and Atlantic oceans, as well as in the Arctic Ocean. It preys on other starfish, such as* Asterias.

symmetrical). Radial symmetry is found much more often in flowers and plants than in animals, and thus one of the wonders of the starfish is the possession of this plantlike shape.

As a matter of fact, starfish do not have perfect radial symmetry. On the upper surface of each starfish and somewhat off center, there is a small spot usually of a slightly different color than the rest of the central disk. This spot, called a *sieve plate* or *madreporite*, is a sort of sieve through which the starfish draws water. Its location somewhat distorts the radial symmetry of starfish, but not much. Some starfish species have more than one madreporite, but these madreporites are not symmetrically located either.

The echinoderms are not closely related to the other "radiate" invertebrates like the jellyfish and coral polyps. The echinoderms

13

originally had a bilateral ancestral form that gave rise early in their evolutionary history to the characteristic radial symmetry seen in the living echinoderms. As far as we know, the jellyfish, and their relatives have always had radial symmetry.

STARFISH SKELETONS

Starfish skeletons are called *endoskeletons* (inner skeletons) because they lie inside the body; they are not *exoskeletons* (outer skeletons), which lie on the outside of the body like the limy shells (skeletons) of snails and clams and the armorlike coverings of lobsters and crabs. They lie just below the outer skin and usually bear spines, hooks, knobs, or tubercles. These hooks and spines and so on are covered by a very fine layer of skin, and they are not nakedly exposed to the air. They consist of a great number of calcareous or limy plates of various sizes and shapes, held together by strong but flexible tissues. Thus, the skeletons are not stiff like snail skeletons (snail shells), but are flexible and can be readily bent, somewhat like chain mail armor.

STARFISH RELATIVES

There are about 1,500 living species of starfish, and they have many close relatives in the sea. These are the sand dollars, the sea urchins, the serpent or brittle stars, the sea lilies, and the sea cucumbers. All these creatures belong to that huge sub-division of the Animal Kingdom called the invertebrates, that is, the creatures which do not have a backbone. Those which do have a backbone, including mammals, birds, reptiles, amphibians, and fish, belong to the subdivision called the Vertebrata, or the vertebrates. In the Invertebrata, the starfish and their relatives belong to a rather large and very ancient group called the phylum Echinodermata or "spiny-skinned" animals (from the

14

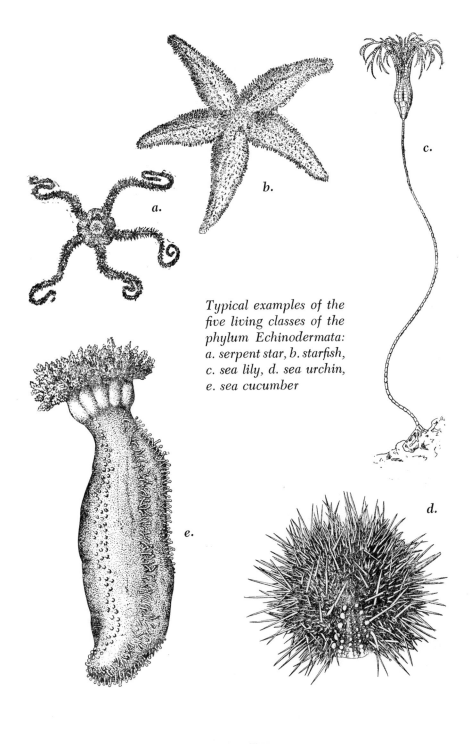

Typical examples of the five living classes of the phylum Echinodermata: a. serpent star, b. starfish, c. sea lily, d. sea urchin, e. sea cucumber

Greek words *echinos*, "hedgehog" or "porcupine," and *derma*, "skin"). They were given this name because many of their members—especially the sea urchins and some starfish—bear long, sharp spines, somewhat like those of porcupines.

CLASSIFICATION OF THE STARFISH

A phylum is usually divided into subgroups called classes, and each class is in turn divided into smaller subdivisions called orders. The phylum Echinodermata consists of five classes, of which the starfish form one class called the Asteroidea (from the Latin word for star). The Asteroidea are divided into several orders. Until about ten years ago, it was generally believed that there were only three such orders called, respectively, the Edged Starfish, the Spiny Starfish, and the Forceps-carrying Starfish. Recently, however, zoologists began studying the distinguishing characters of the starfish larvae and saw so many differences in them and in certain features of adult starfish anatomy that some recognize as many as seven orders. At present there is much difference of opinion among scholars as to how the starfish should be classified. Undoubtedly in the years to come new opinions will appear and old ones will be modified as more studies are

Top view of the shaggy starfish (Odontaster hispidus), a deep-water inhabitant ranging from off Massachusetts to Florida. A member of the order Phanerozonida, it is characterized by the distinctive border formed by the marginal plates. Specimens attain 100 to 125 mm. (4 to 5 inches) in diameter.

made. Under these circumstances the authors of this book have used the conservative classification which recognizes four orders and several suborders of living starfish. We will discuss only the four orders, three of which can be recognized by examining the mature starfish alone, and we will describe briefly the fourth order.

The four orders are the following: The Edged Starfish make up the order Phanerozonida (in Greek this means "visible zones"), and can be recognized because they have a zone or row of large plates along the margins of each arm. In addition they have stiff bodies that are less flexible than the starfish of the other orders. The Spiny Starfish form the order Spinulosida and have, as their name tells us, spiny upper surfaces. These spines are frequently very small, but some, as we shall see later, are quite large and sharp. The Forceps-carrying Starfish, which form the order Forcipulatida, also have spines, but these are always very small and are surrounded by numerous tiny, two-jawed forceps or pincers called *pedicellariae* (from the Latin word for "a little foot"). The pedicellariae play a very important part in

A member of the order Spinulosida, the crown-of-thorns (Acanthaster planci) *is aptly named. This coral-eater inhabits reefs in the western Pacific and Indian oceans.*

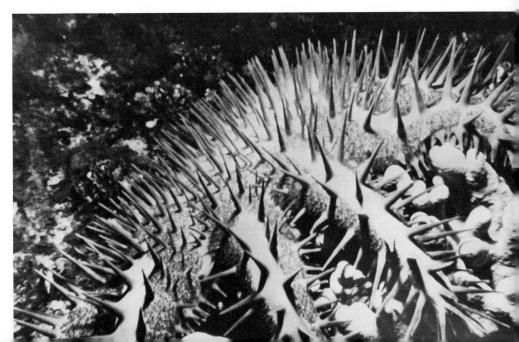

Top view of a starfish (Coscinasterias) *showing the raised pedicellariae on the basal margins of the spines, a characteristic of the order Forcipulatida*

the life of starfish, and we will say much more about them later. Some starfish belonging to other orders also have such pedicellariae, but the pedicellariae of the Forcipulatida differ in being raised on little stalks. In the other species they lie on the surface or sometimes even in little cavities in the skeleton.

The fourth order is called Platyasterida, meaning "flat stars." Until recently, this was believed to be a fossil group whose members had all died out long ago. But some sharp-eyed zoologists realized that at least one family of still-living starfish belonged to the Platyasterida. This family is called Luidiidae, named for a naturalist, Edward Llhuyd. The order Platyasterida is distinguished from the other three previous orders primarily by the strange shape of the larvae, which differ in being longer and having no sucking disk. The larvae in the other orders are shorter and do form a sucking disk to attach themselves to the sea bottom.

There are other characteristics that serve to distinguish the orders of the Asteroidea, but they may be too technical to explain here. However, they are discussed in some of the reference books listed in the bibliography.

A representative of the order Platyasterida, the lingthorn starfish (Luidia ciliaris) *attains a size of 600 mm. (2 feet) across.*

Strange as it may seem, many zoologists believe that of all the major groups of living invertebrates, it is the phylum Echinodermata, including the starfish, that is most closely related to the vertebrates, and hence ultimately to ourselves. Actually the echinoderms are closer to the primitive vertebrates called the protochordates because the protochordate backbone consists of a narrow cord, rather than a column of bones as in the true vertebrates. It is believed that the invertebrate Echinodermata are their close relatives. On what do zoologists base this conclusion? On several important features. They show that the larvae of some echinoderms look very much like the larvae of protochordates. They are so similar that for years the young of of some very primitive chordates were believed to be baby starfish. Though the adult echinoderms and the adult protochordates look very different, the fact that the larvae are similar suggests that the adults are related. In addition, some blood proteins and the nerve chemistry of these primitive chordates and the echinoderms are similar, and the embryos develop in similar ways, very different from other invertebrates like the segmented worms, mollusks, and crustaceans.

In spite of all this it is not correct to say that vertebrates are descended from echinoderms or vice versa. It is more proper to say that both vertebrates and echinoderms may have had a common ancestor that is as yet unknown. Thus the vertebrates appear to be more closely related to the echinoderms than to any other invertebrate group, and starfish might be considered to be distantly related to humans.

3

The Life of Starfish

How Starfish Walk and Climb

Of all the features we find in the Asteroidea, none is perhaps more remarkable than the way they walk, or better, move their bodies along the ocean bottom. Starfish walk on what may be called *water feet*, since watery fluids, forced along by hydraulic pressure, are an important part of the process of locomotion. These water feet are also called *tube feet* because they look like tiny sausagelike tubes. At the end of each tube, there is usually found a small sucking disk, somewhat like those found on the arms of an octopus. The tube feet are arranged in two or four rows along a channel or groove on the lower surface of each arm. The channel is called the *ambulacral groove* from the Latin word *ambulare*, meaning "to walk."

When the starfish has to move from one place to another, liquid is forced into the tube feet. This causes them to become stiff and to reach out, either backward or forward, like narrow toy balloons into which air is being forced. As soon as the suckers at the tips of the tube feet come into contact with the sea bottom or the surface of a hard object, some of the liquid is withdrawn and the muscles of the tube feet create a tiny vacuum at their tips. Thus they are able to adhere to the object. At the same time some tiny glands at the tips of the tube feet suckers give off a

Bottom view of Forbes' starfish (Asterias forbesi) *showing the tube feet arranged in rows running lengthwise along the ambulacral grooves of the arms. The centrally located mouth enters directly into the stomach.*

sticky material which helps the tube feet to cling better. Some starfish species which live on mud or ooze on the ocean bottom do not have suckers at the tips of their tube feet. When their tube feet are extended by the internal water pressure, they are forced into the muddy bottom and cling fast there.

When all the tube feet of a starfish are in position—either clinging to hard surfaces or stuck into muddy or oozy bottoms—the tube feet begin to contract. Then, all together, they pull the entire starfish body forward or backward for a short distance. Now even more liquid is withdrawn from the tube feet, the water pressure is lessened, and each tube foot releases its hold. Then once again liquid is forced in, the water pressure is increased, the tube feet extend, and the whole process is repeated. Thus slowly and steadily the starfish is able to move along.

22

Scientists have studied the speed which starfish can reach. On the average a starfish can cover 15 centimeters (6 inches) in a minute, or 10 meters (about 10 yards) in an hour—providing it keeps in motion that long. However, the starfish that live in the deeper parts of the sea have become adapted to moving a good deal faster because food in the great depths is much scarcer than in shallow waters, and they have to cover greater distances to find something to eat. As a result it is believed that some deep-sea starfish can travel more than three times as fast, or about 30 meters (100 feet) per hour. They cannot reach such speeds by dragging themselves along on the tube feet like their relatives in shallow water. Instead they race over the ocean bottom on the tips of their rays much like a ballet dancer moving over a stage. Many of the deep-water starfish are the kind that lack suckers on their tube feet. But, one wonders how the starfish which do move themselves along on tube feet are able to control the amount of liquid to get each tiny tube foot to move. This is how it is done.

Inside the body of the starfish and around the central disk there is a circular pipe called the *ring canal*. Water enters the ring canal through another short, hard, calcareous pipe called the

Starfish using its tube feet to move over the bottom

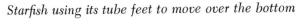

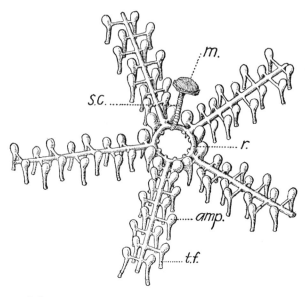

Diagram of the water vascular system of a starfish: m., madreporite; s.c., stone canal; t.f., tube foot; amp., ampulla; r., ring canal

stone canal. The stone canal is connected to a small opening on the upper surface of the starfish body. This opening, the *madreporite,* is provided with a small porous, sievelike cover which serves to filter the water entering the body of the starfish. From the ring canal, five or more pipes run off, one to each of the arms of the starfish. These are called the *radial canals.* Every radial canal has many tiny paired side branches which bring liquid to the tube feet themselves. This system much resembles circular irrigation systems used in arid countries, where a main canal leads to a number of side canals and these to smaller side canals, each of which finally runs into a single plot of ground. The entire system—madreporite, stone canal, ring canal, radial canals, and side canals—is termed the *water vascular system.* It is found only in the starfish and in their relatives of the phylum Echinodermata. The liquid in the system is moved along by tiny waving hairs called *cilia.*

24

Each tube foot has a rounded muscular sac near its own side branch of the radial canal. This sac is called an *ampulla* (Latin for "bottle"), and by expanding and contracting the muscles on the sides of the ampulla, the starfish can push water into the tube foot or withdraw it as needed.

The tube feet are used not only for locomotion; they are also used to bring food to the mouth and to remove undesirable objects. And they help the starfish open the tightly closed valves of a clam or oyster by exerting a steady pull. By using its tube feet, a starfish which has been placed upside down can turn itself right side up. It is fascinating to watch as the active little tube feet reach out one by one to a hard surface and slowly but steadily turn the whole starfish body over.

Zoologists believe that to control each of these thousands of tiny tube feet, the starfish needs to have a very complicated kind of built-in "computer" regulated by the nervous system. Each tube foot in turn has to be directed what to do—how far it has to extend, when to contract, when to rest while pulling on a clam or oyster shell, and when to take over after having rested; when to reach over and take a bit of food or refuse from its neighboring tube foot and when to pass it on to another tube foot. It even has to be informed when to move forward or backward, because as explained earlier, in this radially formed animal, any of the five or more arms can act as the front or back.

How Starfish Feed

Often the most innocent-looking creatures in nature turn out to be among the fiercest. The starfish is one of these. There is virtually nothing living in the sea—provided it is not too fast or too large—dead or alive, that starfish will not attack and eat. They are both scavengers and predators. Even other starfish, often of the same species, fall prey to their cannibalistic brothers. The

25

Stimpson's sun ray starfish (Solaster stimpsoni), *has ten, occasionally nine arms, and reaches 375 mm. (15 inches) across. It lives just below the low tide zone from Alaska to California.*

worst such cannibals can well be the ones called *Solaster*. Their favorite food is other starfish, frequently those of the genus *Asterias*, which are often considerably larger. When it wants to eat, *Solaster* attaches itself to the arm of a convenient *Asterias* and begins to dine. In order to escape from its attacker, *Asterias* quickly casts off the afflicted arm and moves away with the rest of its body. This isn't particularly harmful because the victim soon grows another arm to replace the one which served as dinner for *Solaster*.

But when *Solaster* is considerably smaller than *Asterias*, something remarkable takes place. *Solaster* attaches itself to the very tip of one arm of its victim and begins to push it into its mouth where the digestive juices do their work. Slowly the predator moves up the arm, pushing more and more food into its mouth, digesting all the flesh that it can reach. This goes on for days at a time until the widening taper of the arm becomes too large to fit into the little villain's mouth. Then it lets go and sets off looking for another tip or for a smaller victim. The surprising thing is that the *Asterias*, which must surely feel part of its body slowly disappearing into the stomach of the smaller predator, is unable or unwilling to brush it off. *Asterias* with partially digested arms are not uncommon where *Solaster* abound.

Clams and oysters are favorite food for many kinds of starfish. Anyone who has ever tried to open a clam or an oyster knows how tightly the two valves are held together. How does the starfish get to the delicate meat inside the hard shells? It's a long, slow process. The starfish straddles the food clam and by means of its tube feet turns the prey to a position in which it can be eaten. When the tube feet have become attached with their tiny suction disks to each valve of the clam, they begin a slow and steady pull. They work in relays, some tube feet resting while others keep pulling. Thus the pressure never lets up. This goes on for hours, even days until eventually the poor clam's muscles

A starfish attacking a sea mussel

Several ochre starfish (Pis-aster ochraceus) in the process of feeding on sea mussels. The mussel with the valves open was abandoned after the soft parts were consumed by a starfish.

get tired and the shells open a tiny slit. This is enough for the predator. It is now able to do a very surprising thing. It pushes a sliver of its stomach through its mouth into the opening between the valves and begins to digest the clam's flesh. Recently zoologists discovered that the starfish doesn't even have to wait until the clam's muscles grow tired. The great force (up to 6,000 grams, about 12 pounds), which the predator can apply with its tireless tube feet, is sufficient to bend the clam shell a tiny bit, enough to insert the bit of its stomach and begin digesting the flesh it can reach. This weakens the clam further and the valves spring apart. Now the starfish can push its entire stomach out of its mouth and over the clam meat and digest it all without first swallowing any of it. All it swallows is the digestive juices laden with the liquified food; it doesn't have to take in anything indigestible. Because of this, the starfish do not need elaborate digestive organs to handle waste and finally eject it. They do not have long, complicated intestines, and many starfish do not even have an anus. Practically all the indigestible material is left outside. The highly nutritious, liquified food is then sent on to be further digested by glands located in the arms. All or most all of it is used; there is little if any waste to be gotten rid of.

This is not true of all starfish. Starfish of the genus *Astropecten* (the name means "star comb") do not have suckers at the ends of their tube feet. Thus they cannot, like other starfish, attack clams bigger than themselves by pulling their valves apart. They have to swallow smaller prey which can fit into their mouths. But, if they cannot eat some animals because of their large size, they more than make up for this by eating smaller animals in great quantities. In fact, shell collectors have learned that *Astropecten* stomachs are often good places to look for nicely cleaned but tiny shells. In the stomach of a single *Astropecten* starfish were once found ten scallop shells, six tellin clams, five tusk shells, and several cone shells. Under normal circumstances,

Top and bottom views of the ochre starfish (Pisaster ochraceus), *a common inhabitant of surf-swept rocky shores from Alaska to Mexico, where it feeds largely on sea mussels. Varying from 150 to 450 mm. (6–18 inches) in diameter, specimens occur in yellow, brown, and purple phases.*

after *Astropecten* has had a chance to digest the meat of the mollusks, it expels the empty shells through the mouth.

Sometimes a hungry starfish swallows so much food that its central disk which contains the stomach becomes greatly distended. Another species (*Anseropoda placenta*) with a particularly voracious appetite, nevertheless, shows so little effect from this, that, as one writer says, it seems impossible for any animal to eat so much and to stay so thin.

Shell collectors also find another type of shell in the skin of starfish. This is a tiny, white parasitic snail called *Stilifer* (from the Latin word *stilus*, a "pointed instrument"). It attaches itself to its echinoderm host by a sharp little proboscis (the "stilus" part of its name), much like the proboscis of a mosquito in human skin, and draws off the body juices on which it feeds. There are also a few other kinds of sea snails that parasitize starfish.

As we have seen, nearly everything in the sea can be eaten by starfish. Most commonly, they eat worms, sponges, other echinoderms, and mollusks, but even fish and crabs are relished by some forms of the Asteroidea. It must be hard to imagine how a slow-moving starfish can capture and eat a fast-moving fish. But one scientist saw it happen in a fish tank and described what he saw as follows: "The tail or a fin strikes in its motion the surface of the starfish. At once the rosettes rise, the pedicellariae open, and when the edge of the tail or fin comes against them anew, it is seized by a hundred little jaws. Of course the fish struggles, and in struggling strikes other part of its body against the starfish. Wherever there is a thin edge of fin, tail, or gills, the pedicellariae seize it, and the fish soon finds itself held tightly. Now the tube feet extend, the cruel suckers plant themselves over the smooth surface of the body, and the fish is transported to the mouth. The lobes of the stomach then come forth, press themselves against the tail and proceed to digest it, though the fish still makes at intervals violent efforts to escape. In the course of

A fish captured and held by the tube feet and pedicellariae of a starfish (Stylasterias forreri). During a period of about eight hours, the tail end of the fish was digested and the remainder dropped by the starfish.

six or eight hours, the posterior one-fourth of the body of the fish was usually digested, and the remainder of the fish dropped."

But the prey need not be alive. Dead food, or carrion, is just as welcome to starfish as live-caught food. When a dead or sick fish is very large, two or more starfish may attach themselves to it, and each one digests the parts it can most easily reach. Not all starfish are predators or scavengers. Some live entirely on the tiny animals and plants they filter out of the water. These bits of food are caught on long threads of slimy mucus which are then swallowed. Other starfish ingest large quantities of mud and digest the organic matter found in it. Some are plant eaters only, living off the algae which grow on rocks and other hard objects, even on the glass of fish tanks. Many starfish are practically omnivorous, eating everything in sight, while others are more selective.

The starfish do not have it all their own way. They often have to exert themselves to obtain their food. When a prowling starfish appears in the neighborhood, the reaction of mollusks and other food animals is immediate. Panicky, burrowing clams dig down deeper in the mud or sand, basket snails and cockles leap violently aside, scallops skitter off like frightened butterflies, and fish and shrimp scoot away as swiftly as they can. These animals are first warned by chemical substances the starfish give off in the water and finally by the actual touch of the tube feet. Mollusks, if they cannot run or swim away, defend themselves in different ways. The foot of the abalone shell (*Haliotis*) sends out large amounts of mucus which repels the attacker, then moves away rapidly. Some limpets raise themselves a little from the rocks on which they rest and shake themselves from side to side to loosen any tube feet that may have become attached.

Cockle clams react violently to the presence of predaceous starfish by leaping through the water. The cockle's long muscular foot is extended out of the valves and is snapped back in the opposite direction to move away from the enemy.

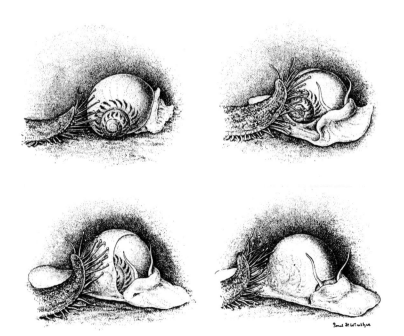

A moon snail reacts to the touch of the tube feet of a starfish by extending a fleshy cape to cover its shell. The starfish cannot grasp the slippery surface, and the snail is able to move away to safety.

This behavior has been called "mushrooming" by animal behaviorists. Other limpets, if they are clinging to a vertical surface, let go and drop to the bottom when a starfish approaches. Dr. James McLean of the Los Angeles County Museum has made use of these limpet habits to collect them. Some very large and strong limpets—some reaching the size of small saucers—live on the coasts of Peru and Chile in South America. These cling so hard to the rocks that it is impossible to get them off without breaking the margins of the shells. Dr. McLean merely puts a starfish, or even a part of a starfish, near a strongly clinging limpet. The startled mollusk gets ready to drop, or flee, or mushroom, and loosens its shell from the rock. A knife can then be slipped under the shell and the animal collected with the shell uninjured.

The moon snail reacts in a very curious manner. It is a slow-

Top and bottom views of the plant-eating Patiria miniata, *sometimes called a "sea bat" because of its webbed rays. It lives on protected rocky shores from Alaska to Mexico. Averaging 125 mm (5 inches) in diameter, these red, yellow, or purple starfish occur in tide pools in great numbers.*

moving creature; it cannot escape readily from the approaching starfish, which is itself anything but fast-moving. Instead, the moon snail draws a thin flap of the foot over its round shell. On this slippery surface the tube feet of the starfish are unable to fix a hold and snail can escape unharmed, if, that is, it can outwait its very patient enemy.

Starfish are persistent; they have to be. Even when a clam digs itself into the sand or mud, it is not always safe. Its enemy can sense its presence even to a depth of 10 centimeters (4 inches). Some kinds of starfish can actually dig their way to their food. The ever-useful tube feet take up the grains of sand one by one, handing them along to their neighbors, eventually expelling the sand off from the tips of the arms. Thus the central disk sinks lower and lower till the unfortunate victim is reached.

Starfish find their food by a strong sense of smell. It was found that a starfish in a tank was able to detect a food fish at a distance of 60 centimeters, almost 2 feet! And another scientist reported that one can lead a starfish around, like a donkey with a carrot, by holding a piece of dead crab five centimeters (2 inches) away from one of its tips. Truly a remarkable feeder is the starfish and an interesting one to watch!

But it is not always easy to observe the starfish's eating process. The starfish hovers over its prey and therefore it is hard to see the stomach being everted, or pushed out. However, the process can be observed easily in the case of one type of starfish called the sea bat (*Patiria miniata*). This is a plant eater and dines largely on algae. In a fish tank with the glass walls covered by algae, one can watch *Patiria* crawling up the glass and see how its everted stomach slowly digests the plant growth away. This also seems to be a good way of keeping the tank glass clean.

How Starfish Breathe

Most of the larger and many of the smaller marine creatures breathe by means of gills. But the starfish have no true gills. They have a simpler and more curious system to take fresh oxygen out of the water and to get rid of the used oxygen. The skeletons of

The smooth Linckia (L. laevigata) *inhabits shallow water in the tropical South Seas. In life, it is a brilliant blue, and the "gills" (papulae) project through the tiny pores that form circular areas scattered over the upper surface. 150 mm. (6 inches).*

starfish are made up of limy plates called *ossicles*. In the spaces between these plates there is room enough for a great number of thin-skinned, blisterlike sacs called *papulae* ("pimple" in Latin). These stick out into the water but can be pulled back when necessary. The membranes of the papulae are so thin that the oxygen molecules in the water can penetrate to the body fluids inside the papulae, and the waste oxygen can be released through them. And so the starfish can breathe. The papulae are usually very tiny and can only be seen under magnification, but there are enough present to satisfy the respiratory needs of the starfish.

How Starfish Reproduce

Starfish are commonly either male or female, *dioecious* (Greek for "two houses") as zoologists say. Very few *monoecious* ("one house") or *hermaphroditic* starfish exist in which each animal is both male and female. Most starfish, especially those living in warmer waters, reproduce by ejecting eggs and sperm into the surrounding water. The eggs are fertilized externally in the water, and the young develop outside the female without any further care or attention by the parents. The eggs are very tiny but they are produced in astounding numbers. The females can produce from 2 million to 100 million eggs each, often several times during a single, rather short breeding season. One zoologist found no fewer than 200 million eggs in the ovaries of a single starfish ready to be released. Sometimes, just before breeding time, well-fed and healthy individuals are so full of eggs or milt that the arms appear to be swollen and rounded instead of flat. By far the greater number of these eggs, of course,

Opposite: *Forbes' starfish grow rapidly during the first four months of life. This illustration (natural size) shows why they are such a menace to oyster farmers.*

never hatch, and of those that do, very few ever reach maturity. But enough are left over, because of their staggering numbers, to make the starfish one of the most numerous creatures in the sea and the bane of oyster farmers.

Many starfish species, especially those living in colder or icy waters, display more parental care. Some, instead of merely shooting their eggs out into the water, deposit them carefully at the bottom of some solid object like a rock. There they are kept in place by a thick coating of mucus laid down by the mother. Other starfish brood their eggs like birds until they hatch, and some often carry the young around on their own bodies until they are big enough to fend for themselves. Some starfish lay their eggs on the sea bottom, then cover them with their bodies, and remain humped over them until they hatch. During this entire time the brooding mother cannot leave to eat; she has to live on the food stored up in her body.

There is one type of starfish (*Odinella nutrix*) of the class Spinulosida that has an even more curious manner of brooding its young. By crisscrossing the spines at the angles where the arms meet the central disk, snug little nests or boxes are formed in which the young safely develop. And finally there are some starfish with the most curious habit of all—they keep the eggs and the young inside a little pouch located in their very active stomachs. Here they stay, safe from digestive juices, until they develop into tiny adults.

An interesting brood chamber is formed in the family Pterasteridae (the name means "wing starfish") which also belongs to the Spiny Starfish order Spinulosida. In this family, the surface of the individual starfish is thickly covered with tiny peglike structures called *paxillae* ("peg" in Latin). Each peg or paxilla has a crown of spines on the top that can be raised and spread out like minute umbrella ribs. When the starfish feels threatened, the little pegs rise and spread out their spines all at the same time. The spines come into contact with each other and thus form an extra protective layer over the starfish skin, a kind of second roof. Thus, the starfish's skin is protected from a shower of annoying sand grains or the attack by tiny animals that might damage parts of the skin. It is in the space between the surface of the starfish and the "second roof" that the eggs are laid, hatched, and the young protected until they fully develop. Thus, what was designed to serve as protection for the entire animal turns out also to be a safe and snug haven for the young. Unlike the others, starfish which brood and shelter their young lay far fewer eggs, varying in number from 5 per brood to no more than 200.

Larval Starfish

The eggs of most of the nonbrooding starfish hatch in from three to four days, and the little free-swimming larval forms emerge. These look quite different from their parents. They are called *bipinnaria* (from the Latin word for "pen" or "feather"). Instead of being radially symmetrical, with the mouth in the center and the arms radiating out in all directions like their parents, they are bilaterally symmetrical, with the mouth at the front end, and the anus at the rear. Because of this fact, zoologists believe that the starfish originally did not possess a radial form, but

A bipinnaria larva of a starfish (greatly enlarged). Note the bilateral symmetry.

are descended from some bilateral ancestor. The bipinnaria larvae are usually tiny, but in one species (*Luidia sarsi*) they can reach a size of 35 millimeters or 1⅖ inches.

The larvae swim around freely, sometimes for as long as twenty days. Finally they develop a tiny suckerlike organ with which they attach themselves to some hard underwater object. At this stage they are called *brachiolaria* from the Greek word meaning "forearm." In about twenty-four hours they undergo a complete change, the little larva turning into a slow-moving, radially symmetrical, young starfish. In the case of the brooded eggs, there is no free-swimming larval stage; the eggs hatch and the larvae develop inside the eggs or in the mother's brood case.

We do not know too much about the life span of starfish. Some are known to live for five or six years, but apparently most kinds only survive for three or four years.

Although most starfish, as we have seen, are either male or female, it is not easy to tell the sexes apart, since externally their bodies are very similar. One has to cut the animal open and

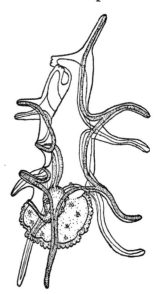

A brachiolaria, the free-swimming larval stage of a starfish (greatly enlarged)

examine the reproductive organs, located in each of the arms, to see whether they contain eggs or milt.

The methods of reproduction described above are the normal ways in which most starfish reproduce. They are called *sexual reproduction* methods because both sexes, male and female, play a part. But a few kinds of starfish can also reproduce asexually, where the sex organs play no part. In one type (*Coscinasterias* in Bermuda), the animal is somehow able to tear itself in two pieces, dividing across the central disk. Each piece retains a part of the disk and some of the arms. In time, each partial disk regenerates completely and the missing arms are replaced to the normal number. Then we have two starfish where we had one before. Until the starfish are completely re-generated, they are a queer sort of animal with some large and some small or tiny arms. At this stage, they do not look very symmetrical, radially or otherwise. But that soon changes and a normal-looking starfish eventually is formed.

Another type of starfish in the genus *Linckia* has an even more interesting way of splitting itself when it reproduces. It is able to break off its arms, one at a time. This casting off takes three to four hours to complete, the arm literally tearing itself away from the rest of the body. When it is loose, the arm sets about developing its own central disk and other arms, sometimes as many as nine. Finally it turns into a full-fledged mature starfish which can, in its turn, reproduce by sending off one of its own arms. While the new arms are developing and are still very small, the starfish looks not like a star in the sea but rather a comet. It has a long tapering "tail" and a "head" formed by the tiny arms at the wider, torn end. Zoologists do indeed call this the "comet" form. As a result of this constant splitting off of arms and growing of new ones, very few *Linckia* specimens are alike. One observer reported that of four hundred specimens, only four were at all alike, the others showing one to nine arms as well

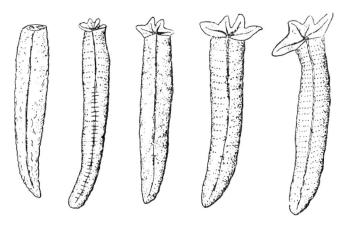

Development of the "comet" form of a regenerating starfish

as other distinctive differences.

Some species of starfish can also throw off their arms rapidly, but they do this in order to escape from their enemies, not for reproduction. The English naturalist Edward Forbes in 1841 reported what happened to him when he was trying to collect large, living specimens of what he named *Luidia fragillissima* (now known as *Luidia ciliaris*). This is the starfish the English fishermen call "the lingthorn." Forbes wrote, "Never having seen one before and quite unconscious of its suicidal power, I spread it out on the rowing bench, the better to admire its form and color. On attempting to remove it for preservation, to my horror and disappointment, I found only an assemblage of rejected members." On another occasion, a specimen he was trying, with a great deal of care, to remove from a dredge, began to "dissolve his corporation, and at every mesh of the dredge his fragments were seen escaping." Little wonder that Forbes chose the name *fragillissima* for this species; the word means "most fragile" in Latin. Several other species can also do this, but not quite so dramatically.

42

We have seen that starfish can be active predators which kill and eat anything of convenient size. But, as everywhere in nature, they are often themselves victims of other hungry carnivores. Sometimes they are eaten by other starfish. The eggs and larvae are devoured by the billions by all sorts of animals, and many species of fish feed on injured adult starfish and eat vast numbers of young starfish. Crows and gulls pick them off rocks, but only when other more desirable food is not available. There are even some tiny crustaceans which settle on the starfish skin and peck away at the delicate papulae which serve as "gills" or breathing tools for the starfish. These, we suppose, can be as annoying to a starfish as fleas to a dog. Other crustaceans form gall-like cysts in the skin of starfish in which they spend their lives.

Against these and other predators the starfish have some effective defenses. Against the larger predators they are more or less protected by their tough, rough, or spiny surface, against smaller ones by a host of little pincerlike organs called *pedicellariae* (from the Latin word for "little feet").

The pedicellariae are really modified spines. They usually

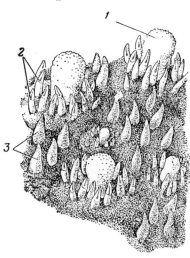

Portion of the upper surface of As-terias rubens, a member of the order Forcipulatida, much enlarged. 1. denuded base of a spine, 2. pedicellariae raised on stalks, 3. breathing papulae.

consist of two parts controlled by muscles so that they can close and catch hold of minute objects, dead or alive. Some pedicellariae are shaped like pincers or forceps in which the two blades are joined at one end and which close directly when pressed together. Other pedicellariae operate like scissors or pliers in which the two blades are crossed like an X and pressure is applied at the extended handles. Often the blades of the pedicellariae are toothed to provide a firm grip on anything they catch hold of. Although most starfish have pedicellariae, there are some primitive species in the order Spinulosida which do not. Instead their bodies are protected by a thick covering of closely set spines.

The pedicellariae are arranged in groups at the base of the spines. When a curious crustacean or other kind of pest goes exploring over the skin of the starfish, it is quickly caught by one pedicellaria. This pedicellaria then passes it on to its neighbor and so on until it is finally thrown off over the edge. By that time most likely the pesky intruder is no longer alive. Pedicellariae also do this to get rid of sand grains and other foreign debris. And, as we have seen, they help catch fish. Thus, they can be

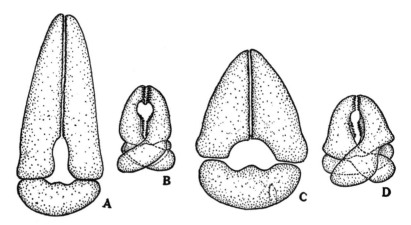

Pedicellariae much enlarged. The "pincer" type (a and c); the "scissor" type (b and d).

looked upon as a sort of defense and sanitation squad, in addition to their food-gathering duties. Later we will describe an experiment which you can perform with the pedicellariae of a live starfish.

The upper surface of the starfish is also kept clean by cilia or hairs which keep waving and thus wash away tiny particles of dirt. Many starfish species, especially in the order Spinulosida, also have a way of protecting their mouths and ambulacral grooves in which the tube feet are located. Starfish cannot close their mouths the way we do. Nor can they close the ambulacral grooves for protection. Instead, along the edge of the mouth and the ambulacral grooves there are rows of strong, rather large, movable spines. Usually these spines stick straight out, but when the starfish is disturbed, it can depress the spines so that they rest across the mouth and the grooves. Thus a strong fencelike cover is formed to protect the soft tissues within the mouth and the delicate tube feet inside the ambulacral grooves.

There are many other natural forces that destroy starfish in large numbers. Sudden and sharp temperature changes of the water can kill many starfish as can sudden, overwhelming rainstorms which lower the salt content of the water. Many starfish are killed by rolling stones or pebbles, and huge numbers are left to die and dry on the shore by stormy waves, much to the delight of beachcombers. And finally there is man, especially the oyster farmer, who tries to control the starfish that feast on his oyster beds.

The most effective means the starfish have against becoming endangered species—besides the huge numbers of eggs they can lay—is their amazing power of regeneration, that is, the ability to replace parts of their body that have been cut or torn away or otherwise injured. We have seen this power of regeneration in the case of the asexual reproduction of the starfish genus *Linckia*, where an arm can literally tear itself away from the rest of the body and in time form an entirely new starfish.

Now, other creatures also have the power of regeneration. Some lizards cast off their tails and grow new ones. Crabs that have lost a pincer or leg can replace it when they moult. In all these, and many other cases, only a small part is replaced. But rarely in nature can so much grow back from so little as in the starfish. A single arm of a starfish with a bit of the central disk attached can grow into a complete animal, arms and all.

Before they knew better, oyster farmers would chop up any starfish they caught on their oyster beds and throw them back into the sea. Little did they realize that many of these chopped up pieces survived to regenerate normal individuals. Thus, instead of getting rid of many starfish pests, they merely increased their numbers. Now the oyster farmers are wiser. They throw them into vats of boiling water to kill them.

It is important to realize that, unlike *Linckia*, most starfish species must have at least one arm and a section of the central disk before regeneration can take place. An arm alone usually dies, as does the central disk if all the arms are removed. Scien-

A "freak" starfish in the process of regenerating. Notice the forked tip of one of the main arms.

tists have also discovered that when all the tube feet are cut away from one of the arms, the starfish throws off the damaged arm and grows a new one. It merely grows a new arm to replace such an injured one. But when the tube feet are lost as a starfish is torn off a rock, they are replaced by newly grown ones. In such cases, the detached tube feet continue to cling to the rock by themselves, and they have been found to live like this for several days. But they themselves cannot regenerate and grow into a new starfish.

Regeneration is not a very fast process. In some species it takes more than a year to replace a lost arm completely. It probably takes even longer when one arm, plus the central disk, develops all the missing parts. Thus, the "comet" form, of which we spoke earlier in the section on reproduction, remains the comet form for a long time before it turns into a "star."

Frequently, the process of regeneration is interfered with. When this happens all sorts of starfish freaks and monsters result. Thus we find starfish that normally have five arms with four, six, or even more arms. Sometimes one of the arms is split at the tip so that it grows out forked. At other times, instead of one madreporite or sieve plate, there are several. Zoologists have performed some strange experiments on starfish which have resulted in even more bizarre forms. Any normal starfish in the process of regeneration will look very much like a freak. But given time, it will turn into a more or less normal form. But these accidental or artificial freaks remain so until they die.

The Senses of Starfish

We have already seen that starfish have a rather good sense of smell to find their food. It is also known that they are aware of lightness and darkness, as they feel their way along the ocean bottoms.

Where do these senses lie? Starfish have a circular nervous system with branches into the arms and the tube feet. These nerves control the various activities of the tube feet by directing each one what to do. Here must lie the "computer" which we have already mentioned. There is also a thin netlike layer of nerves which lies just below the outer skin. These nerves control the tiny organs we described earlier—the papulae or "gills," the pedicellariae or "pincers," and the paxillae or "umbrella pegs" where such are present. In addition, at the tip of each arm there are a few tube feet that do not have suckers at the tip. These are the tentaclelike sense organs that help detect chemical substances in the water. They attract the starfish to odors that promise food and enable them to avoid odors that might alert them to harm, like the "smell" of an enemy or the presence of polluted water. They might also signal the animal when a starfish of the other sex is near so as to begin the breeding process. And finally, at the tip of each arm in most starfish there are also small cushionlike areas, usually of a different color. Here are located clusters of tiny, simple eyes called *ocelli*. The eyes can

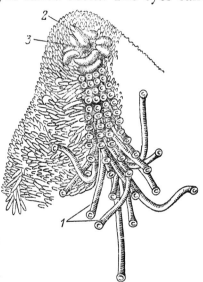

Tip of an arm of Asterias rubens.
1. tube feet in various degrees of extension; 2. sensory tentacles; 3. ocelli or eyes.

The netted starfish (Oreaster reticulatus) *is common in shallow water on grassy and sandy bottoms from Florida to Brazil and attains 200 mm. (8 inches) from tip to tip. Note the raised arm at the bottom right with ocelli examining the surrounding water.*

probably see no more than the difference between light and dark. Starfish have been seen to lift the tips of the arms as though to let the ocelli search the waters around them.

With all these senses, are starfish very smart? Not very, we must conclude on the basis of experimentation. They seem to be able to work their way out of some difficult situations, like freeing themselves when their arms are fastened together with rubber bands. But they don't seem to learn much as they do this; they don't remember the ways out of problems they solved. They repeat all the old errors over and over again. Apparently, it would be quite useless to try to teach a starfish any tricks. However, starfish don't seem to need to learn very much. They are doing very well as it is.

49

4

The Coral Reef Killers

In 1960 on Green Island in the Great Barrier Reef of Australia, a strange round, flat, spiny creature was discovered on the coral reef. It was about 60 centimeters (23 inches) in diameter, of a dull reddish brown color, and had at least twelve arms fixed to a central disk. It was obviously some kind of starfish. Soon scientists identified it as the crown-of-thorns, a rarely found species, with the scientific name *Acanthaster planci*, meaning "the thorn star of Planc." Wherever the starfish were observed on the living coral, they left a large bare spot. It was soon discovered that these starfish devoured the coral polyps and left only the dead coral skeleton where they had feasted. A few years later, tourists in glass-bottomed boats were startled to see thousands of *Acanthaster* moving over the reefs at Green Island. They were killing vast numbers of coral colonies and devastating huge areas of the reef. In 1966, the crown-of-thorns were found in great numbers in Guam, almost two thousand miles away, and there also they were destroying the reefs.

About this time similar alarming reports were coming in from many other coral islands in the western Pacific Ocean, including the Hawaiian Islands. The populations of crown-of-thorns starfish were exploding, and huge areas of coral reefs appeared to be in great danger of being killed. Interestingly enough, most

Several crown-of-thorns starfish (Acanthaster planci) *on a coral reef at Madagascar, where they have eaten the coral polyps and only the white skeleton of a coral head remains. Note the darker, living coral head on the left.*

populations of this starfish in the Indian Ocean and Red Sea, as well as those of a closely related species in the tropical eastern Pacific, were not found to be abnormally large.

Nevertheless, a kind of panic set in. Several governments spent large sums of money and sent out many expeditions to study this menace and find a remedy. The inhabitants of the coral islands saw disaster staring them in the face. They were afraid that if the reefs died, the fish and other reef-inhabiting animals would vanish. The loss of this protein-rich food supply might lead to starvation. There appeared to be an even greater danger. Many of the oceanic islands on which people live are located inside lagoons protected from the force of the open ocean by surrounding or fringing coral reefs. If the starfish succeeded in killing the coral animals, the reefs would stop growing. Little by little they would be reduced or worn away by wave action. In a short time the inhabited islands, deprived of their coral reef protection,

51

would be destroyed by storms and heavy seas. The homes of many thousands of people and the very land on which they were built would vanish, washed away by the sea.

The *Acanthaster* proved to have another unpleasant characteristic. Their strong, sharp spines appeared to be poisonous. People who accidentally stepped on them or whose fingers were pricked by the thorns, developed painful symptoms, which lasted for hours. Altogether, the crown-of-thorns was an unwelcome creature.

Up to the time of its discovery on Green Island Reef, *Acanthaster* had been rarely seen on the reefs. As a result, very little was known about it. But scientists soon learned a great deal. Like most starfish, the crown-of-thorns extrudes its stomach through its mouth, surrounds its prey, and digests it. The scientists were able to find out more about its biology. Although *Acanthaster* has only a very short breeding season, every female starfish two years and older can produce 12 to 24 million eggs! No wonder it had reproduced so rapidly without adequate natural controls. They also discovered that the spines themselves were not poisonous; it was the thin outer skin covering the entire skeleton of the starfish that was toxic to humans. Many other facts were discovered, but scientists were looking for some means of controlling the exploding populations of *Acanthaster*. How could they fight it?

Poisons were ruled out immediately. Their use would probably kill large numbers of *Acanthaster*, but would also destroy most if not all the other reef inhabitants. The result might have been that man would be as much a reef killer as the starfish. As a matter of fact, some scientists believed man had caused the original decline of the corals by interfering with the natural environment of the coral reefs. In some places, ship channels had been blasted through the reefs, and corals had been removed to use as lime for cement.

52

How about natural enemies? The investigators found very few. The most effective one was the large triton shell called *Charonia*. This sea snail was able to insert its snout between the sharp spines, pierce the hard outer skin with its filelike teeth, and eat the soft internal flesh of the starfish. *Charonia*, however, also preys on sea urchins and sea cucumbers as well as other starfish and it even seems to prefer these to *Acanthaster*. Fortunately, where large concentrations of the crown-of-thorns occur, these snails were found to kill many of them. Moreover, it was discovered that the crown-of-thorns could move faster than the triton and thus many escaped it. Some shrimps and crabs were also found to prey on the starfish, but obviously these natural predators had failed to control the starfish once they had developed to adult size.

Although each female starfish is capable of producing millions of eggs in its lifetime, few of them survive the larval stage to attain maturity. Many of the eggs and the larvae are eaten by the very coral polyps which later themselves become victims of the grown-up *Acanthaster*. Without healthy corals to consume them, too many of the larvae will survive and eventually overpopulate the reefs with starfish. Thus, when men began destroying coral reefs to form ship channels and to obtain lime for building materials, they may have unknowingly contributed to the rapid growth of crown-of-thorns populations.

Scientists had to devise artificial ways to control the adult starfish. SCUBA divers descended to the reefs and either collected the starfish by hand and removed them from the sea, or injected a shot of formaldehyde into each one to kill it. These means were more or less effective in some areas, but they were not the solution of the problem.

As time passed, little by little the danger seemed to lessen. Perhaps the efforts of the scientists had finally begun to have results. Or more likely, the *Acanthaster* population explosion had

53

A diver wearing heavy protective gloves injects a solution of formaldehyde into a crown-of-thorns starfish.

come to a natural end, as it usually does in other animal species when a natural balance is restored. New coral growths began to appear on the dead corals and the reefs began to revive. But not all coral species are returning with the same speed; some species show up quickly, others will take a longer time. It will require, some scientists estimate, between ten and twenty years for all the reefs to recover completely. Because we did not know enough about the ecology of the coral reefs and their associated plant and animal life, apparently we over-reacted to what now appears to be a natural cycle of population expansion and decline—one that had not been observed for this species in the past.

5

Starfish and Mankind

STARFISH AS FOOD

It is strange that although starfish are so abundant in shallow water in many parts of the world, mankind has made so little use of them except in minor ways, such as wall decorations and as souvenirs of seashore trips. As a matter of fact, it was not until 1733 that the first treatise dealing solely with starfish appeared in print. This interesting book was written by John Henry Linck, a druggist living in Leipzig, Germany.

No human beings, it seems, have ever learned to use them regularly as part of their diet as they have clams, snails, crabs, shrimps, and even seaweeds. This is probably due to the fact that starfish are mostly "skin and bones" without much meat and even that little meat doesn't taste very good. Because the eggs or roe of sea urchins, close relatives of the starfish, are widely relished, especially along the Mediterranean coast, it was thought that starfish roe could be similarly eaten. We know of one man who tried eating them mixed in scrambled eggs. He reported that he ate the dish with no ill effects but also without much pleasure. Besides, there is a certain amount of danger, since it is known that the roe of some starfish is poisonous. It appears that even primitive people did not eat starfish, apparently for very good reasons.

Starfish do not even appear very often in myths and super-stitions. Because they resemble the stars in the sky, some people believed that starfish actually fell from the heavens and lived on in the sea. The English poet James Montgomery hinted at this idea:

> The heavens
> Were thronged with constellations, and the seas
> Strown with their images.

In Ireland, starfish used to be called the Devil's Fingers or the Devil's Hands, and the children were afraid to touch them. Among the oyster farmers of the Breton coast of France, starfish are believed to be the wicked fairies. The good fairies, "by the grace of God," are the stars which remained in the sky; the wicked ones were cast out of heaven like Lucifer and his fallen angels. The halibut fishermen of the British Isles used to look upon some kinds of starfish as good luck charms. Before starting to fish, they placed a live starfish, which they called "the butthorn" (*Astropecten aranciacus*), into their boats. If the fishing trip turned out to be good, the starfish was returned to the sea with thanks. If it was poor, the "seastar" was allowed to dry up and perish in the boat.

The inshore fisherman of the East Coast of the United States believe that if a starfish is in a lobster pot, there will be no lobsters. Most likely this is not a superstition but a fact based on sound observation. The presence of a starfish is probably enough to discourage a lobster from trying to get to the bait in the pot—if, as a matter of fact, the starfish hasn't eaten the bait first.

Starfish were also thought to be good medicine against hernias, perhaps because the extended stomach of a feeding starfish some-

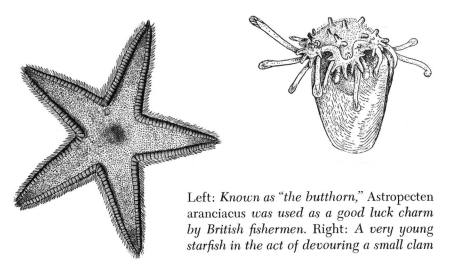

Left: *Known as "the butthorn,"* Astropecten aranciacus *was used as a good luck charm by British fishermen.* Right: *A very young starfish in the act of devouring a small clam*

what resembles a hernia. In ancient times starfish were boiled in wine and the mixture used as a remedy against epilepsy and hysteria. If any of these remedies actually worked, it was probably due to the power of suggestion. However, since important antibiotics and other medicines have recently been found in clams, snails, and even sponges, it is not impossible that in time a valuable drug will also be dicovered in starfish.

STARFISH AND OYSTER FARMERS

While mankind has never learned to make much use of them, starfish have made excellent use of one of man's important activities, the cultivation and harvesting of oysters. We have seen that bivalves, clams, scallops, and oysters are a favorite food of starfish, and carefully tended oyster beds provide them with an easy source of food. Many years ago, starfish practically ruined all the oyster beds in Long Island Sound. In 1958 they were accused of causing a loss to oyster farmers of between 10 and 15 million dollars, and as recently as 1976, in spite of all efforts to control them, starfish proved again to be a serious menace not only, this time, to the oyster crop, but also to the yield of bay scallops.

Although starfish prey on oysters all around the world, it is only in the shallow waters of the northeastern shore of the United States that they are a serious menace, especially in the centers of oyster cultivation such as Buzzards Bay in Massachusetts, Narragansett Bay in Rhode Island, Long Island Sound in Connecticut and New York, and Chesapeake Bay in Virginia. The most harmful species is the common Forbes' starfish (*Asterias forbesi*) which is found from Maine to Florida, but in largest numbers from Cape Cod to Virginia. The purple starfish, *Asterias vulgaris*, is also a menace, but because it lives in deeper water and appears in smaller numbers, is not so great a pest as *A. forbesi*. Both species belong to the forceps-bearing class of starfish, the Forcipulatida.

It is true that the poor oyster farmer has to contend with many other hazards to his crop, such as underwater mud slides, a multitude of diseases, various parasites, numerous boring organisms (sponges, mollusks, bryozoans, and barnacles), fouling organisms, and finally other predators including snails and crabs. But the starfish are the most destructive of all. One reason is that the young starfish settle and begin to forage for food just before the settling time of the oyster spat. The result is that when the oysters are ready to settle, they have to compete for space with hungry young starfish that are ready and eager to eat up all the oyster spat they can reach. Thus a new oyster crop can be completely destroyed before it has had any chance to grow.

Not only the young or the spat of the oysters are attacked by starfish; many larger ones are also destroyed. Some scientists state that a single starfish can consume as many as five one-year-old oysters in a day. Others tell us that a starfish can eat fifty-six oysters as long as its arm in six days. And the starfish can appear at a single locality in tremendous numbers. At times layers of starfish as much as eighteen or twenty inches deep can be seen to extend in bunches and masses over large areas of bottom, each one a deadly menace to the oyster farmer's crop. In 1929 one oyster-raising company removed 10 million adult starfish from its oyster beds in Narragansett Bay!

Nor are the starfish satisfied with devouring the oysters of a single oyster bed. When one bed has been depleted, they move along to another. They do not always have to pull themselves along on their tube feet. In Long Island Sound underwater photographs have been taken of starfish curling up the tips of their arms, releasing their hold, and floating along just above the bottom, carried by the strong tidal currents. When the currents slacken at the turn of the tide, the starfish fall to the bottom and find themselves in new localities. Here they begin to hunt immediately for food. Thus, an oyster bed, which might just have been cleaned of starfish, can be invaded again in a very short time.

It is hard to imagine how, under such conditions, any oyster farmer can stay in business very long. Fortunately for him, starfish do not appear in large numbers every year. They may be abundant for a year or two, followed by a period when they are scarce. When starfish appear in very large numbers, many oystermen think that this is due to new invasions of starfish from other areas. But in 1939, a young marine biologist named Victor L. Loosanoff proved that periods of abundance are caused by an unusually large number of starfish larvae surviving and reaching maturity. This can be due to warm winters and other factors. Another biologist named A. D. Mead suggested a method the farmer might use to lessen the chances of this happening. This procedure can be used after a particularly mild winter when a starfish population explosion can be expected. As we know, when the larvae or bipinnaria of the starfish are ready to settle, they attach themselves chiefly to fluffy, branching seaweeds. In a

59

single handful of seaweed Dr. Mead once found more than one thousand young starfish. Thus if the seaweed at low water mark can be collected in large quantities before the young starfish are big enough to move to the bottom and attack the young oysters, millions of the larvae can be destroyed and the numbers of young starfish considerably reduced. This method of control does not seem to have been widely used, perhaps because many other organisms, including the seaweed, are destroyed as well.

What else can the oyster farmer do to protect his crop from starfish attack? One of the most successful and most widely used methods is by working with a starfish mop, also called a tangle. This consists of an iron bar, eight to ten feet long, held horizontally. From this bar twelve to sixteen light iron chains with five-foot-long bunches of unravelled rope yarn are hung at regular intervals. The bar with the chains and rope yarn is dragged from a boat across the infested oyster bed. When the starfish come in contact with the mop, they seize the fibers with their pedicellariae or simply become entangled in the meshes. The mop is then brought on board, and the starfish dumped in a vat of boiling water and destroyed.

A boat equipped with two starfish tangles hanging from booms on the stern

In addition to this mechanical method of controlling starfish, there is also a cheap, efficient chemical method. Quantities of quicklime (calcium oxide) are poured over an oyster bed. When it comes into contact with starfish, it burns large wounds into the surface of the animal and it soon dies. Even if the lime doesn't kill the starfish quickly, they are so weakened by the wounds that crabs, fish, and other animals attack, kill, and eat them. The lime has two advantages: it does not dissolve very rapidly in the water and thus stays effective for a long time, making its use less expensive; and even more important, it does not have any adverse effect on the oysters and the other animals in the water that have protective shells or scales. But it may harm the soft-bodied creatures, like sea anemones and most worms.

Other methods of combatting starfish have also been used. One of these is the suction dredge. This works like a large underwater vacuum cleaner which sucks up the animals and mud from the bottom. The material is then shaken through rotating drums with wire mesh that lets the mud and smaller objects fall

61

through. The larger animals are then deposited on a conveyor belt, the starfish and other oyster pests are picked off and destroyed, and the oysters are either harvested or returned to the bed to grow to a larger size. This is a very efficient method of both harvesting the oysters and controlling the starfish and is much used by the larger oyster farming companies.

Still another method is to dip the oysters in strong solutions of common salt as they are being transferred in dredges to other areas. Starfish die when they are immersed for only thirty seconds to a minute, and many other oyster enemies, large and small, also

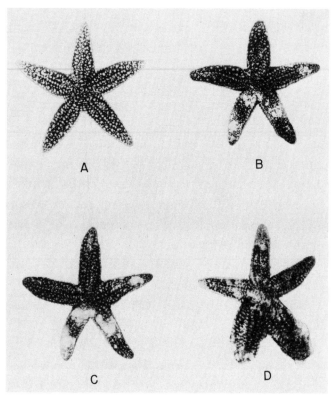

Lime is an effective means to control starfish on oyster beds; a. an untreated specimen, b–d., specimens demonstrating progressive stages of injury after contact with particles of lime

perish. Some organic poisons have also been used, but they were found to be more effective against oyster drills than against starfish.

Very recently a new product has appeared on the market which may prove to be a successful means of preventing starfish attacks on oysters. This is a plastic mesh made by DuPont and called Vexar. So far it has been widely used to package oranges and other fruits in food markets. Young oysters can be put into these bags and the bags returned to the oyster bed. Here the oysters hopefully will grow to marketable size inside the bags, and at the same time the Vexar keeps the starfish away. The plastic material does not decay in the salt water. The oyster farmer who uses the mesh can place his oysters wherever he wants to and still be sure that they are safe from starfish predation.

Nowadays more and more oysters are being grown experimentally in aquacultural laboratories rather than in the natural environment of bays. When these artificial methods are perfected, starfish will cease to be a menace to the oyster farmer and a threat to those of us who love to eat oysters. As a result, we will be able to appreciate better the wonders of the starfish without having to worry about the harm they might have caused our commercial fisheries.

THE USES OF STARFISH

For a while it was thought that dead starfish could also be used to fertilize crops or to use as meal for poultry feed. Oystermen hoped that they had another source of income in the starfish which they regularly cleaned out of their oyster beds and killed. But this did not work out very well. Not enough starfish were produced and the oystermen soon found that it didn't pay to save them for the farmers. Now the starfish are merely killed and dumped overboard.

Two kinds of predatory snails known as oyster drills

Are starfish any use to mankind at all? A newspaper story reported that "the starfish have no known function in the marine chain of life." This, of course, is not true. In the form of sperm, eggs, and larvae, which, as we have seen, starfish can produce in vast numbers, they provide a great amount of food for other creatures, even for the oysters and clams which other starfish will later try to eat. In addition, the starfish even help oystermen by eating other harmful predators like oyster drills. They also keep down the population of slipper shells which compete with the oysters for food and often are so numerous that they actually suffocate the oyster spat.

Starfish are also beneficial to the economy of the sea because they act as some of the most important marine scavengers and thus help keep the seas free of dead and decaying organisms. Finally, it must stated to the credit of the starfish class that they are one of the few larger animal groups that do not have members which have degenerated into parasites. They are such a successful group of organisms that none of them has had to evolve a parasitic form of life, as have some crustaceans, mollusks, worms, and others.

6

Working with Starfish

HOW TO PRESERVE STARFISH

Starfish for the most part are easily preserved. Those found thoroughly dried by the sun on a beach can make satisfactory specimens. But to prepare the best specimens for a starfish collection, some simple steps should be taken. The live specimen should first be placed in a flat-bottomed pan containing sea water and then relaxed (narcotized) by adding a sprinkling of Epsom salts (magnesium sulphate) to the water. When the specimen is completely relaxed, fresh water is then added to the container gradually until it completely replaces the sea water. When the specimen is dead, it should be placed in a 70 percent solution of alcohol and left there for several hours. Rubbing alcohol, which can be purchased in any drugstore, is satisfactory for this use. In order to retain the strength of the alcohol, it should be changed once or twice after a day or two. Finally, the specimen can either be preserved permanently in a 70 percent solution of rubbing alcohol, or if preferred, removed from the alcohol and dried by artificial heat. Small specimens are easiest to preserve in alcohol, for they do not require much space to store. Such specimens can later be dissected for anatomical studies, or examined under a microscope. More commonly, specimens are dried for purposes of display or for reference collections. Neither method satisfactorily preserves the pigments, most of which are lost when the specimen dies. Thus, it must be admitted that a collection of preserved and dried starfish, though it is very interesting, is not colorful. However, color photographs can be taken of living or fresh specimens and kept for reference.

Some people use artificially colored starfish for wall decorations and for various kinds of ornaments. The following procedures are recommended: The starfish are washed in fresh water, arranged in baking pans and flattened out with the arms evenly spread. The pans are then placed in a slow oven (150° to 200° F.) until the specimens are completely dry. Or, if you don't mind the odor, they can be dried in a hot sun, provided they are covered with cheesecloth or otherwise protected from flies and other vermin. Once completely dry, the starfish can be spray-painted in any desired colors by the use of spray guns or aerosol spray cans.

Starfish stranded on a beach after a storm and exposed to the elements by a receding tide

A collection of dried starfish, representing nine genera: 1. Patiria, *2.* Solaster, *3.* Linckia, *4.* Pycnopodia, *5.* Astropecten, *6.* Pisaster, *7.* Patiriella, *8.* Oreaster, *9.* Luidia

IDENTIFYING STARFISH

Most starfish can be easily identified and named. The members of the order Phanerozonida (the Edged Starfish) and the Spinulosida (the Spiny Starfish) usually can be quickly recognized—the former by the presence of the "visible zone" of plates edging the margins of the arms and by the rather stiff and inflexible body, the latter by the presence of a rough and spiny upper surface and a more pliable body. The Forcipulatida (Forceps-carrying Starfish) can be definitely identified only by careful observation of the pedicellariae. In this order the "pincers" are fixed to little stalks which raise them above the surface. As far as the order Platyasterida is concerned, most members of which are extinct, it is represented by the living family Luidiidae. More restricted identification to family, genus, and species can be most readily made by referring to the pictures and

67

descriptions in this and other books on starfish. This task is made much easier by keeping in mind the place where the specimens were collected, since many books limit themselves to describing and illustrating the starfish of certain areas (see the bibliography).

Once a specimen has been identified, the scientific name should be written on a label together with the common or English name if such exists. The label should also bear other data such as the exact locality where collected, type of bottom—that is, the substrate—on which the starfish was found, the date and time of day when collected, the names of plants and animals found nearby, and additional observations like the behavior of the starfish just before it was captured—for instance, "taken while it was trying to pull the body of a sea snail out of its shell." Such a collection, conscientiously maintained and neatly arranged, would make not only a fascinating and instructive hobby, but also a valuable addition to the knowledge of the starfish fauna of a restricted area and a collection which any museum would be proud to own.

Observing Starfish

Starfish are easily kept alive for a long period of time in a well-aerated saltwater aquarium. Unless the aquarium is very large, it is best not to keep more than one starfish at a time. If there are more than one, they might try to eat one another. All the normal precautions for keeping an aquarium healthy and well-running must be taken. There are many books that explain how to maintain a saltwater aquarium. One of the best of these is *Marine Aquarium Keeping* by Stephen Spotte and is listed in the bibliography.

Starfish make interesting pets, and one can enjoy watching them and recording their activities. Among other things, one

Various ways starfish use to right themselves

can observe them opening the valves of a clam and digesting the meat by means of their pushed-out stomachs. The tube feet can be watched in action, and, under magnification, the workings of the pedicellariae and paxillae can be seen. Specimens can be turned over and observed as they right themselves.

They accomplish this task in three different ways. A great many starfish simply curl the tips of one or two of their arms under until their tube feet can seize hold of the bottom. Then the feet slowly push ahead until the entire animal is turned over in a sort of somersault. Other starfish use more elaborate methods. Lying on their backs, they raise their arms so that they look more or less like a flower with upstanding petals. This position is, indeed, called the "tulip" position by biologists. Eventually, the starfish rolls over to one side, the arm on the bottom curls over, its tube feet grasp the bottom, and slowly the animal rights itself. Some starfish use just the opposite way to right themselves. Instead of raising their arms, they bend their arms to the bottom and raise the central disk like a human gymnast doing a backbend on the floor. Eventually, they either roll over, or the tube feet on one or two of the arms are able to seize the bottom and turn the animal over. It has been noted that it takes starfish from two to ninety minutes to right themselves. You might make some interesting discoveries by carefully timing your starfish pet. You will find a starfish kept in a clean, healthy tank to be as interesting to watch as a lively fish.

EXPERIMENTING WITH STARFISH

As we have seen, most starfish are either male or female. However, it is not possible to tell what sex any individual specimen is by merely examining the exterior. Male and female starfish look essentially alike. To sex the individual properly, you must be willing to sacrifice the specimen. First of all you must find a "ripe" specimen, that is, one which is ready to shed its eggs or sperm. On the northeast coast of the United States, May or June is the best time to collect them. Now you must relax the specimen as we described above until it has become narcotized. To test whether the animal is narcotized and has become numb, you should probe the tube feet and see if they react to your touch. Then, with a pair of dissecting scissors, the top, hard surface is removed from one of the arms. This is best done while the specimen is under water. Now, with a pair of fine forceps, the featherlike sexual glands, which are uncovered when the outer surface is removed, are gently lifted and shaken in a basin of water. If a milky cloud escapes, the specimen is a male. The "cloud" is a mass of millions of sperm cells. If instead of a cloud, a tiny stream of particles like sand grains barely visible to the naked eye flows out, the specimen is a female and the particles are the ova or eggs. For further proof, if any is needed, a droplet of the water containing the sex cells can be observed under a high-power microscope. Later, in order to make sure that the animal was not deprived of its life simply to satisfy your curiosity, the dissected body should be preserved in alcohol for future study. You might later want to make other anatomical observations on this already-dissected specimen. On the West Coast, when the sea bat (*Patiria miniata*), a common intertidal starfish

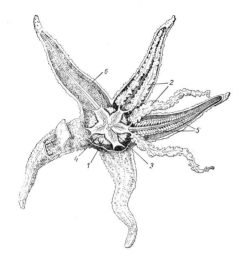

A dissected specimen of Asterias rubens with upper surface partially removed.
1. stomach, 2. digestive glands,
3. anal gland, 4. madreporite
and stone canal, 5. ampullae
of the tube feet, 6. gonads
(sexual glands).

species, is laid out on wet seaweed, a large percentage of male and female specimens will discharge their ripe sperm and eggs almost throughout the year, especially in the winter months. Thus the parent animals can be sexed and returned to the sea unharmed. With care these eggs can be fertilized and the young raised for further observation. It takes only a single night for the fertilized eggs of this species to transform into microscopic larvae, and under ideal conditions they will eventually develop into young starfish.

With patience and over a long period of time, one can even watch a starfish regenerating a lost arm. One arm is carefully removed with a sharp scalpel a little above the central disk and the animal placed in the tank. The wound heals and a small bump, the beginning of the new arm, appears. Slowly it grows in size until, usually in about a year, the starfish has completely replaced the missing arm. If this experiment is to be performed properly, it is necessary to keep a careful record in the form of a "regeneration diary." In such a diary or journal the steady growth of the new arm is measured and recorded every few days together with such information as the type and quantity of food eaten, the temperature of the water, and any other information.

Since starfish regenerate so readily, all sorts of oddities can be created, as we have seen in the chapter on reproduction. Arms can be grown which are split in two near the tip, or the number of arms can be artificially increased. Such experiments should be undertaken very carefully and at sufficient intervals of time so as not to weaken the starfish unduly and cause it to die.

An even simpler experiment can be performed with the pedicellariae of a live starfish: Take a healthy specimen of one of the larger starfish such as *Pisaster* or *Asterias* and allow the upper surface to rest against the naked skin of your forearm or leg. After a few seconds lift it away; you should feel a series of sharp nips, for the tiny pincers of the pedicellariae have become attached to the surface of your skin. Or, if you are less adventurous, try the classic experiment using writing chalk. Drop some crushed chalk on the top of a starfish. The pincers of the pedicellariae will immediately go to work and grind the chalk into a fine powder. These particles are then removed by the waving microscopic cilia that cover the surface of the starfish.

We hope that after having read this introductory account of the wonders of starfish, you will want to know more about these remarkable creatures. You can learn more by reading the books we list in the back and others which might catch your interest. But the best way of learning about them is, as we have said earlier, to observe them as they go about their daily activities either in well-kept aquarium at home or, even better, in their natural surroundings at the seashore. You might be able to see something that even starfish experts have not seen before. Such things have happened in the past and no doubt will happen again in the future, and new facts may be added to our knowledge of natural history by your own patience and persistence.

Glossary

ambulacral groove—am-bu-*lack*-ral, a furrow extending from the mouth into each arm of starfish, generally containing two to four rows of tube feet and commonly guarded by movable spines that are able to cover the groove

amphibians—am-*fib*-ee-ans, animals able to live on both land and in the water, like frogs, salamanders, etc.

ampulla—am-*pull*-a, the rounded, muscular, bladder- or blisterlike sac that connects with a tube foot of a starfish at the radial canal; pl. ampullae

arthropods—*ar*-thro-pods, the "joint-footed" animals belonging to the phylum Arthropoda, including the insects, crustaceans, spiders, etc.

bilateral symmetry—characteristic of a body or part that can be divided on a central plane into equal right and left halves, each a mirror image of the other

bipinnaria—by-pin-*nar*-ee-a, the first stage of starfish larva

bivalve—*bi*-valve, a class of mollusks comprised of those with two shells, like clams and oysters; the class Bivalvia

brachiolaria—brack-ee-o-*lar*-ee-a, the fixed larval stage attained by some starfish; the stage following the bipinnaria form

bryozoans—bry-o-*zo*-ans, tiny moss animals belonging to the phylum Bryozoa

calcareous—cal-*car*-ee-us, composed of or containing calcium carbonate; limy

carnivorous—car-*ni*-vor-us, eating or living on the flesh of animals

chordates—*cor*-dates, animals belonging to the phylum Chordata, including the vertebrates and protochordates (tongue worms, tunicates, ascidians, and lancelets); generally characterized by the presence, at

73

some stage of life, of a stiff cord which, in the adult stage, is lost in some chordates and in others is replaced by the backbone

cilium—*sill*-ee-um, a tiny hairlike process attached to the surface of a cell and generally capable of vibration; pl. cilia

class—a category in the classification of plants and animals, ranking between a phylum and an order; e.g., class Asteroidea

crustaceans—crus-*tay*-shuns, members of the arthropod class Crustacea, including crabs, lobsters, shrimps, barnacles, isopods, copepods, etc.

dioecious—dye-*ee*-shus, having the male and female organs in separate individuals; sexes separate

echinoderms—eck-*eye* (or-*ee*) -no-derms, representatives of the phylum Echinodermata, including starfish, brittle stars, serpent stars, sea urchins, sand dollars, sea biscuits, sea lilies, sea cucumbers, etc.

ecology—the relationship of an organism to its environment

endoskeleton—an internal skeleton

exoskeleton—an external supporting structure or shell covering of arthopods, mollusks, and some other invertebrates

fertilization—the union of an egg cell and a sperm cell which begins the process resulting in the development of an embryo

genus—*gee*-nus, a group of related species which form a subdivision of a family; pl. genera

gonad—*go*-nad, a reproductive organ within which the ova (in females) or the sperm (in males) are produced

intertidal zone—the transition area from the sea to the land that is alternately covered and uncovered once or, more commonly, twice daily by the tides

invertebrate—in-*ver*-te-brate, any animal without a dorsal column or a cordlike support for the body

larva—*lar*-va, the early stage of an animal, after the embryo and unlike the adult; pl. larvae

limpet—*lim*-pet, a marine mollusk with a nonspiral, caplike, snail shell

limy—consisting of or containing lime or limestone; see calcareous

madreporite—*mad*-re-*pore*-ite, the sievelike plate on the top of the starfish that filters the water entering the body of the starfish and connects with the stone canal of the water vascular system; also called "sieve plate"

milt—the product of the male reproductive gland; see sperm

mollusks—animals belonging to the phylum Mollusca (meaning "soft"), including snails, clams, oysters, squids, octopuses, etc.

monoecious—mo-*nee*-shus, having both male and female gonads in the same individual; hermaphroditic

ocelli—*o-sell*-ee, the tiny eyes at the arm tips of most starfish

omnivorous—om-*ni*-vor-us, eating all kinds of food, both plant and animal

order—a category in the classification of plants and animals, ranking between a family and a class; e.g. order Spinulosida

organism—a single plant or animal

ossicle—*os*-sickle, one of many small limy plates of various sizes and shapes arranged in a meshwork and bound together by tissues and muscle fibers to form the skeleton of a starfish

ovum—*o*-vum, the female sex cell; an egg; pl. ova

papula—*pa*-pyou-la, soft, branching organs that project from the body cavity and between the spines in starfish and serve as gills; pl. papulae

parasite—*par*-a-site, an organism living on or in another organism at the expense of the host

paxilla—*pax*-ill-a, a peglike structure projecting from the skin of some species of starfish, with a crown or rosette of spines that can be raised and expanded like the ribs of a tiny umbrella; pl. paxillae

pedicellariae—pe-*dis*-ell-*ar*-ee-a, small pincerlike or scissorlike spines, often toothed, that occur in the spaces between the spines or in clumps around the base of spines on the skin of some echinoderms

phylum—*fye*-lum, the chief division in the classification of the Animal and Plant kingdoms, e.g. the phylum Echinodermata

polyp—*po*-lip, an individual animal of a coral that builds the coral skeleton; also the soft body of a coelenterate (see-*len*-ter-ate), "hollow-gut animals," often grouped together to form colonies

population—a group of individuals belonging to a single species living in a given time at a given location

predator—an animal that preys upon other animals for its food

radial canal—the tube in each arm of starfish that connects with the central ring canal of the water vascular system

radial symmetry—similar parts arranged around a common central axis, as in starfish

radiate—having rays or radial structures; organisms characterized by radial symmetry, such as sponges, corals, jellyfish, and echinoderms

regeneration—replacement of parts lost through mutilation or otherwise

ring canal—the circular pipe of the water vascular system in starfish which connects with the stone canal and from which the radial canals extend

sea anemones—a-*neh*-mo-nees, flowerlike sea animals related to corals, sea fans, etc.

shellfish—a term loosely applied to the "shelled" invertebrates, especially the edible mollusks and crustaceans

sperm—the male sex cell

stone canal—the limy tube that connects the madreporite to the circular ring canal of the water vascular system of starfish

substratum—sub-*stray*-tum, an ecological term denoting where an organism lives, e.g. rocks, sand, mud, etc; also called "substrate"

symmetrical—divisible into equal and opposite parts; see bilateral and radial symmetry

tellin—a type of handsome marine bivalve; the genus *Tellina*

trematodes—*tre*-ma-toads, a class of flatworms including the blood flukes and their allies

tube feet—the hollow, thin-walled cylinders commonly, though not always, ending in suckers, that are attached to the side branches of the radial canals of the water vascular system of starfish

tubercles—small, knoblike bumps or protuberances

vertebrate—*ver*-te-brate, an animal having a segmented backbone or a vertebral column; see chordates

water vascular system—the unique hydraulic pressure mechanism of echinoderms that functions primarily as a means of locomotion. The word *vascula* means "a small vessel" in Latin.

Annotated Bibliography

Barrett, John H., and C. M. Yonge, 1958, *Collins Pocket Guide to the sea shore*. Collins, London.

The commonly found British starfish are briefly described and are illustrated in color.

Buchsbaum, Ralph, 1948, *Animals without backbones*. University of Chicago Press, 2nd edition. Starfish treated on pp. 300–309.

A clear and not too technical discussion of the asteroids, excellently illustrated. Not for identification of species.

Buchsbaum, Ralph, and L. J. Milne, 1967, *The Lower Animals*. Doubleday, Garden City, New York. Echinoderms treated on pp. 254–285.

Contains magnificent color illustrations of some common starfish species with brief discussion of the class.

Clark, Ailsa M., 1962, *Starfishes and their relations*. British Museum, London.

A helpful general survey of echinoderms, with special reference to those found in North European waters.

Coe, Wesley R., 1972, *Starfish, serpent stars, sea urchins, and sea cucumbers of the northeast*. Dover Publications, New York. Originally published in 1912 as *Echinoderms of Connecticut*.

Contains authoritative descriptions of the commoner starfish of the northeastern coast of the United States and adjacent areas. The nomenclature is dated.

Downey, Maureen E., 1973, *Starfishes from the Caribbean and the Gulf of Mexico*. Smithsonian Contributions to Zoology, no. 126, Washington, D.C.

An excellent, definitive, rather advanced treatment of the starfish of the region; useful for identification of species.

Fechter, H., [in] B. Grzimek, 1974, Animal Life Encyclopedia, volume 3, chapter 14, pp. 361–388, Van Nostrand-Reinhold, New York.

Brief but clear discussion of the starfish, provided with magnificent color illustrations.

Forbes, Edward, 1841, *A History of British starfish*. London.

A charming account of the starfish of the British waters by one of the fathers of the study.

Furlong, Marjorie, and Virginia Pill, 1972, *Starfish*. Ellis Robinson Publishing Co.

A useful identification guide to the starfish of the Pacific Coast of North America; includes details on methods of preserving starfish.

Gray, I. E., M. E. Downey, and M. J. Cerame Vivas, 1968, *Sea-stars of North Carolina*. Fishery Bulletin, volume 67, no. 1.

A fine account of the commoner starfish of the region; useful for identification of species.

Hyman, Libbie Henrietta, 1955, *The Invertebrates*, volume 4, *Echinodermata*. McGraw-Hill, New York.

A thorough, technical account of the phylum by one of the leading American zoologists of the century; not for identification of species.

Moore, Raymond C., editor, 1966, *Echinodermata* [in] *Treatise on invertebrate paleontology*, Part S, volume 1, 1967, part U, volume 3, 1966. University of Kansas Press.

A comprehensive, if quite technical, treatment of the phylum, down to genus and subgenus only; superbly illustrated.

Nichols, David, 1962, *Echinoderms*. Publishers, Ltd., Hillary House, New York.

A useful general survey of the living representatives of the phylum; not for identification of species.

Ricketts, Edward F., and Jack Calvin, 1968, *Between Pacific Tides*. Fourth edition, revised by Joel W. Hedgpeth, Stanford University Press, Palo Alto, California.

Contains many references to West Coast starfish.

Spotte, Stephen, 1973, *Marine Aquarium Keeping, the Science, Animals and Art*. John Wiley & Sons, New York.

Explains how to keep starfish in an aquarium, pp. 78–80.

Tubiash, Haskell S., 1966, *Ornamental Use of Starfishes*. U.S. Department of the Interior, Bureau of Commercial Fisheries, Washington, D.C., Circular Number 253.

Explains how to prepare dried starfish for use as attractive ornaments.

Index

Numerals in **boldface** refer to the captions to the illustrations.